Action Sports

Kickboxing
The Modern Martial Art

Daniel Sipe

Capstone Press

MINNEAPOLIS

Printed in the United States of America.

Capstone Press • 2440 Fernbrook Lane • Minneapolis, MN 55447

Editorial Director   John Coughlan
Managing Editor   John Martin
Copy Editor   Theresa Early
Editorial Assistant   Michelle Wood

Library of Congress Cataloging-in-Publication Data

Sipe, Daniel, 1969-
　　Kickboxing / Daniel Sipe.
　　　　p. cm.-- (Action Sports)
　　Includes bibliographical references and index.
　　ISBN 1-56065-203-9 (lib. bdg.)
　　1. Kickboxing--Juvenile literature. I. Title. II. Series.
GV1114.65. S57 1994
796.8' 15--dc20   93-40643
                                                                    CIP
                                                                    AC

ISBN: 1-56065-203-9

99 98 97 96 95 94   8 7 6 5 4 3 2 1

Table of Contents

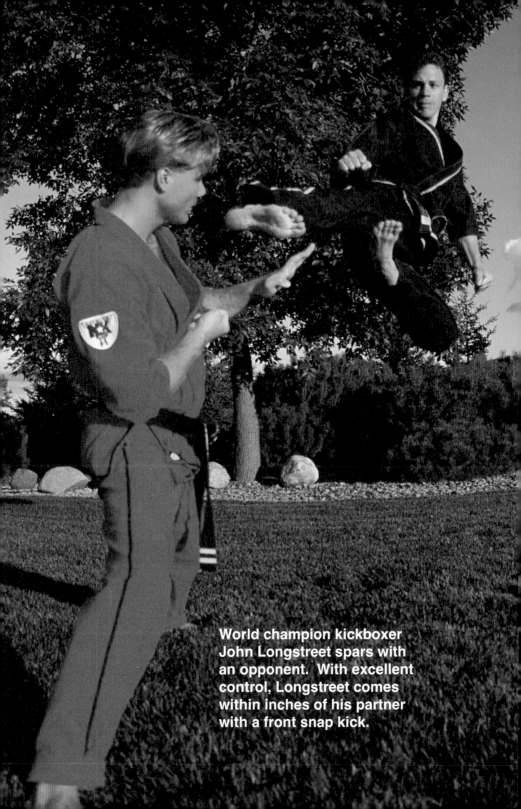

World champion kickboxer John Longstreet spars with an opponent. With excellent control, Longstreet comes within inches of his partner with a front snap kick.

Chapter 1

Ancient Art and Sport of the Future

Kickboxing is a cross between boxing and the traditional **martial arts**. Imagine a sport that combines the incredible kicks of Bruce Lee and the powerful fists of Sugar Ray Leonard. Together, these skills make up the leaps, kicks, and spinning fists that kickboxing delivers.

In a kickboxing match, contestants score points with both their hands and feet. The action is fast.

Bruce Lee, probably the
most famous martial artist of

With so many ways to get hit, kickboxers have to be smart, too. Kickboxers spend much of their time practicing ways to block and dodge oncoming attacks. Speed, not power, is the key to effective kickboxing.

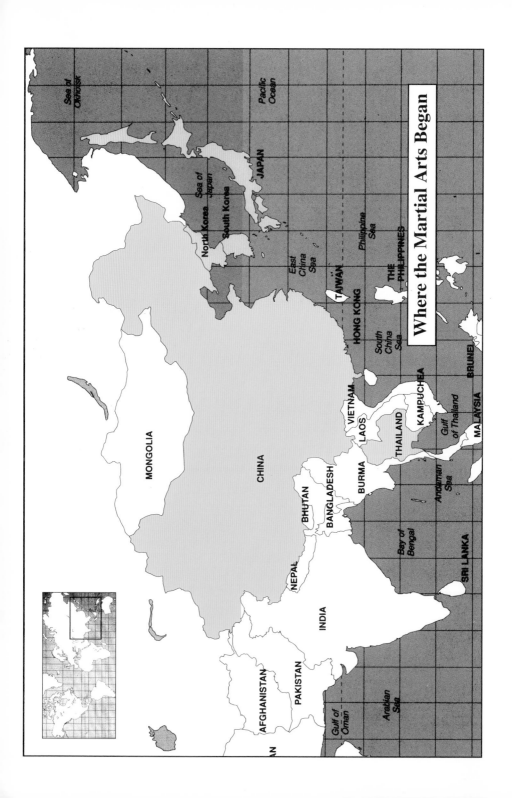

Where the Martial Arts Began

Chapter 2

The History
of Kickboxing

Kickboxing is a new sport that comes from a very old tradition.

The Asian Martial Arts

The kicks used in American kickboxing are drawn from ancient martial arts of the Asian countries, including Korea, China, Japan, and Thailand (see map).

Thousands of years ago, Asian warriors discovered that the human body could be used as a weapon for both attack and defense. Through disciplined practice, they trained their bodies to twist and flex. Over many years, they perfected their kicks, and learned to explode into quick bursts of power.

Karate

American kickboxing comes from karate. Karate is a Japanese method of combat that doesn't use weapons. The word *karate* means "empty hand."

When karate first came to the United States, it was a non-contact sport. Fighters won points for accurate near-misses, not for hits.

But to many people, winning a karate match without touching an **opponent** seemed wrong. They liked the contact sport of judo. In a judo match, you earn points by throwing or holding an opponent down.

Athletes began to change karate. They looked at boxing, where the goal is to knock your opponent to the ground. They looked at wrestling, where the goal is to pin the opponent's shoulders to the mat. And they came up with something new.

Full-Contact Karate

In the 1960s Jhoon Rhee, a karate teacher, developed a new style of fighting that used both hands and feet. This was known as full-contact karate.

This sport used the punches and blocks of the European sport of boxing. Full-contact karate and American kickboxing mixed this European sport with Asian moves.

Quick Popularity

From the very beginning, full-contact karate was very popular. Both athletes and spectators loved the speed, action, and style of the sport.

In 1973, an American named Mike Anderson organized the first full-contact karate tournament. The tournament was a great success.

More and more athletes practiced the sport. It soon became clear that full-contact karate was not just another form of karate. It was a new sport altogether. It was the beginning of American kickboxing.

The First Kickboxing Stars

The new sport attracted some great fighters, like Joe Lewis and Chuck Norris, the quick-punching movie star. Later came Bill "Superfoot" Wallace, a fighter whose kick was as fast as his punch, and the Canadian Jean Yves Theriault.

Still later came the Belgian fighter Jean-Claude Van Damme and Benny "The Jet" Urquidez, stars of many kickboxing movies.

Two of the more important kickboxers to fight in recent years are Dennis Alexio and Kathy Long. Dennis Alexio was the men's world heavyweight champion. Kathy Long, women's world featherweight champion, became one of the sport's most popular athletes.

American kickboxing is now one of the most popular martial arts. Thousands of amateur and professional athletes compete as

12

The boxing Belgian, Jean-Claude Van Damme

kickboxers. Millions of fans throughout the world enjoy the sport in live matches and tournaments, on television, and in films.

Chapter 3

Basic Equipment

Kickboxing has a full set of rules on what a boxer must wear during a match.

Female kickboxers wear karate suits, which include a pair of baggy drawstring pants, a wrap-around jacket, and a cloth belt. Male kickboxers do not wear the jacket or belt.

Gloves

The Karate International Committee of Kickboxing, Inc. (KICK) sets rules about clothing and gear. According to KICK rules, kickboxers must wear boxing gloves.

Gloves come in two weights. Professional kickboxers who weigh 152 pounds (68.9 kilograms) or less must wear 8-ounce (227-gram) gloves. All amateur kickboxers, and professionals who weigh 152.1 pounds (68.9 kilograms) or more, must wear 10-ounce (284-gram) gloves.

When punches and kicks are flying, quality safety equipment is a must.

Foot Pads

For safety reasons, kickboxers must wear foot pads made of foam covered with a vinyl casing. Soft surgical bandages are wrapped around the pads and held in place with adhesive tape.

Headgear

KICK rules require amateur kickboxers to wear leather headgear. The headgear covers the ears and protects the head from blows.

Other Protective Gear

Boxers must use fitted mouth guards to protect their teeth and wear shin pads of a soft material. Male kickboxers wear protective groin cups.

Taking a class is the safest
way to learn kickboxing.

Chapter 4

Getting Started

The only way to be successful in kickboxing is through hard work and dedication. This book can show you only a few moves. To really learn kickboxing, you must attend a class. A teacher can correct your mistakes, and you can practice with other students in the class.

Stretches

Because tight muscles are easily injured, kickboxers stretch their muscles with warm-up exercises. This helps make their muscles limber.

To prevent injury, it is a good idea to stretch out before a kickboxing session.

Stances

The first lesson in kickboxing is how to stand. Each stance is a balanced and flexible position.

The Front Stance

For the left front stance, the right foot is placed behind the left. The feet are slightly more than shoulder width apart. The left foot points at the opponent. The right foot points slightly to your right. Most of the weight is on the front foot.

Both arms are bent and the hands are held in front of the boxer.

The right front stance is a mirror image of the left front stance.

The front stance

The back stance is much like the front stance, but your weight is on the rear foot. It is easier to kick from this stance.

The Back Stance

For this stance, the feet are slightly more than shoulder width apart. This stance is very similar to the front stance, but most of the weight is on the rear foot.

The Side Stance

The boxer stands with the feet one-and-a-half to two shoulder widths apart. The toes point in slightly. The boxer's weight is evenly divided over both feet. The fists are at hip level or a little higher. The boxer turns his or her head toward the opponent.

Chapter 5

Basic Moves: Kicks, Punches, and Blocks

Kicks are offensive moves in kickboxing. The kicks used most often are the side kick, the front kick, and the roundhouse kick.

The kicks can only be briefly outlined here. The best way to learn correct kickboxing moves is a class.

The Side Kick

Kickboxing's basic kick is the side kick. This kick can be both a great offensive weapon and a powerful defensive move.

To throw a side kick, the boxer starts in the

In a side kick, the kicking foot sweeps around from the outside and strikes the opponent's body or head.

side stance. While bringing one knee up to his or her waist, the kicker holds the foot up and out to the side. Next, he or she snaps the leg out towards the opponent. The whole leg should be firm and straight when the blow lands.

The side kick is a stunning defense against punches. Because your legs are longer than your arms, the side kick can stop almost any punch.

The Front Snap Kick

The boxer starts the front snap kick from the right or left front stance. If the athlete is in the left front stance, he or she lifts the right knee toward the waist. Then the boxer quickly

A student demonstrates a front snap kick while sparring. This kick came within inches of the opponent but did not strike him. Until you develop some skill, you should not practice kicks on another person.

snaps the foot towards the target. Once the blow is delivered, the boxer snaps his or her foot back to the ready position, then returns to the front stance.

From the right front stance, the left leg is used.

The Roundhouse Kick

The roundhouse kick is a snap kick. The ball of the boxer's foot strikes the opponent.

Standing in the front stance, the boxer

Roundhouse kicks deliver a solid blow with a quick snap.

brings the right bent leg up to a position parallel with the floor. This brings the foot near the hip. The athlete then pivots on the left foot. At the same time, he or she swings the right leg to the front. The knee stays high.

The boxer then snaps the right leg outward and brings it around while finishing the pivot. The kick is delivered in a snapping movement.

The boxer brings the foot quickly back to the hip. This can be done from either stance and with either foot.

Punches

The punches used in American kickboxing come mainly from the sport of boxing. Commonly used punches are the straight punch and the jab.

Good kickboxers do not throw wild punches. That means no swinging punches or side-arm punches. Wild punches are easy to block.

Punches can be delivered with either the right or left arm. A good kickboxer's punch comes from the whole body, not just the arm.

The Straight Punch

This punch is usually aimed high at the opponent. The boxer starts in the front stance, then snaps the front fist toward the target. Just before the blow lands, the boxer turns the fist inward. At the same time, the boxer twists slightly to bring the chest into line behind the blow.

The boxer quickly pulls the fist back to the ready position.

The Jab

The jab begins in a back stance. The punching hand is pulled back slightly, toward the hip. The boxer shifts forward into a front stance and twists the punching hand inward as the blow lands. By moving forward into the blow, the boxer adds much power to the punch.

Blocks

The kickboxer uses blocks to defend against kicks and punches. Two popular blocks are the lower block and the inside center block.

You can perform these blocks with either arm.

The student on the left blocks a straight punch and delivers a jab to her opponent.

By practicing your timing, you should be ready to quickly return a punch at the end of each block.

The Lower Block

The lower block is used most often to block attacks against the lower part of the body. It is a simple but strong one-two move.

Standing in a left front stance, the athlete bends the left elbow, bringing the left fist up along the right side of his or her neck. Next, the boxer straightens the arm downward. Extending the arm fully lets the outside of the arm block the kick.

The block finishes when the boxer brings the arm again to the bent position, with the fist against the right side of the neck.

The student on the right defends himself with a lower block against a kick.

During the inside center block, the raised fist moves from the inside to the outside. This directs any punches or kicks away from the body.

The Inside Center Block

Standing in a left front stance, the boxer moves the left fist across his or her chest. The athlete points the fist straight upward, directly above the elbow. The arm can then be swung outward to push any blow away from the body.

Chapter 6

Kickboxing Competition

Once you have mastered the basics of kickboxing, you can begin to compete.

Amateur and professional kickboxers compete in as many as 17 weight classes. Male and female kickboxers compete separately. Male weight classes range from flyweight–112 pounds (50.8 kilograms) and under–to super-heavyweight–more than 205 pounds (93 kilograms).

Rounds

KICK has set official rules for kickboxing matches. Each round is two minutes long with a one-minute rest between rounds.

Most matches generally have no fewer than five rounds and may have as many as 12 rounds.

The Ring

Matches take place in a ring at least 16 feet (5 meters) square. Padding covers the floor of the ring and extends over the edge of the platform. Three or more ropes line the ring.

The Referee

A referee enforces the rules. He or she is there to make sure the play is fair and to guard the safety of the boxers.

The kickboxers bow to the referee and then to each other before the match begins.

The Judges and Points

A match has three judges who award the contestants points for each round. The judges give 10 points to the boxer who shows the most effective kickboxing in each round. From one to nine points go to the other fighter, depending on the ability they showed.

John Longstreet, World Kickboxing Champion

Kicking Requirements

In every kickboxing round, each boxer must use a certain number of kicking attacks. A professional kickboxer must deliver eight kicks each round. Amateurs must perform six kicks per round.

If a boxer does not make the required number of kicks in two rounds, he or she loses points.

There is a reason for this rule. Punches are easier to land than kicks. Without the **penalty**, boxers might use only punches. The match would become a boxing match, not a kickboxing competition.

Knockdowns

When a boxer is knocked down or falls down on purpose, the referee starts an official countdown. If the boxer does not stand up by the count of 10, the referee awards the match to the other boxer.

In a match, a boxer who is knocked down three times in a round loses.

Fouls

All moves used in karate, kung fu, tae kwon do, and other martial arts are allowed in kickboxing competitions.

However, many moves are illegal. They include kneeing, biting, spitting, head-butting, jabbing the opponent's eyes, and grabbing or holding the opponent's leg. If a boxer uses an illegal move, the referee calls a **foul**. The contestant loses two, three, or five points depending on the foul.

Fouls can cause a boxer to be **disqualified**, meaning he or she is not allowed to finish a match. For a serious foul, a boxer can even be **suspended** from the sport of kickboxing and not allowed to compete at all.

It is a good idea to use a punching
bag while practicing kicks.

Chapter 7

Kickboxing Safety

As you try out your new kickboxing moves, be sure to do them safely. Stretch your muscles slowly before you begin. Use movements that extend your muscles gently but thoroughly. It is important to be loose when you begin.

Use protective mats on the floor. They will cushion any falls so you aren't injured.

It's best to learn from a teacher, in a kickboxing class. There you will learn many more moves, and you can practice regularly with a **sparring partner**.

Never hit your sparring partner. Remember,

While sparring, take care not to injure your opponent and always wear safety equipment.

kickboxing is a sport. It is wise to stop your blows at least one inch (2.5 centimeters) before they would hit your partner. Practice strikes, punches, or kicks against a punching bag, not a person. Hit an opponent only when you are physically attacked.

Avoid doing anything that could hurt your partner. You might want to develop a signal between you and your partner to let each other know if one if you gets injured.

Glossary

disqualified–not allowed to finish a match; the opponent wins.

foul–an illegal move, such as a jab at the opponent's eyes

martial art–any form of traditional Asian self-defense or combat with weapons

Muay Thai–traditional Thai boxing, similar to American kickboxing

opponent–a person who is on the other side in a game or contest

penalty–a punishment given to someone who breaks a rule or law

shadowboxing–punching at the air, or at your "shadow"

sparring partner–an opponent in practice who helps to train a fighter

suspended–not allowed to compete for a certain time

To Learn More

About martial arts:

Brimner, Larry Dane. *Karate*. New York: F. Watts, 1988.

Neff, Fred. *Karate is for Me*. Minneapolis: Lerner, 1980

——. *Lessons from the Western Warriors: Dynamic Self-defense Techniques*. Minneapolis: Lerner, 1987.

Pulaski, George R. *Action Karate*. New York: Sterling, 1986.

Queen, J. Allen. *Fighting Karate*. New York: Sterling, 1988.

——. *Karate Basics*. New York: Sterling, 1992.

About kickboxing:

Baltazzi, Evan S. *Kickboxing: A Safe Sport, A Deadly Defense*. Rutland, VT: Tuttle, 1976.

Index

Photo Credits:

Acknowledgments

The publisher would like to thank John Longstreet and National Karate Schools. Their contributions have been invaluable.

A special thanks to these students at National Karate Schools for their help: Jessie Benson, Jenny Cook, Otis Smallwood, and Collin Mullin.

The publisher also wishes to thank the following organizations for their help with the book:

K.I.C.K Productions, Inc.
2940 Westwood Blvd., Suite 1
Los Angeles, CA 90064

Karate International Council of Kickboxing
1251 Ferguson Avenue
St. Louis, MO 63133
(314) 727-8232

Frank Babcock, Commissioner